*This journal belongs to*

..............................................................................................

# The Beauty of Motherhood

Most of all the other beautiful things in life come by twos and threes, by dozens and hundreds. Plenty of roses, stars, sunsets, rainbows, brothers and sisters, aunts and cousins, comrades and friends—but only one mother in the whole world.

KATE DOUGLAS WIGGIN

Ask any four-year-old boy, "Who's the most beautiful woman in the world?" His mommy! Ask any grown daughter caring for her aging mother the same question, and you'll get the same answer.... Moms spend a lifetime humbling themselves in taking care of others. Nothing is more attractive.

LISA WHELCHEL

Therefore, as God's chosen people, holy and dearly loved, clothe yourselves with compassion, kindness, humility, gentleness and patience.

COLOSSIANS 3:12 NIV

To be a child is to know the joy of living.
To have a child is to know the beauty of life.

# The Wisdom of a Child

For the wisdom of the wisest being God has made
ends in wonder; and there is nothing on earth so wonderful
as the budding soul of a little child.

LUCY LARCOM

Kids: they dance before they learn
there is anything that isn't music.

WILLIAM STAFFORD

And the Spirit of the LORD will rest on him—
the Spirit of wisdom and understanding....
In that day the wolf and the lamb will live together....
And a little child will lead them all.

ISAIAH 11:2, 6 NLT

The greatest poem ever known
Is one all poets have outgrown:
The poetry, innate, untold,
Of being only four years old.

CHRISTOPHER MORLEY

A child can ask questions that a wise man cannot answer.

..........................................................................................................

..........................................................................................................

..........................................................................................................

# Spread the Joy

As we grow in our capacities to see and enjoy the joys that God has placed in our lives, life becomes a glorious experience of discovering His endless wonders.

Since you get more joy out of giving joy to others,
you should put a good deal of thought into
the happiness that you are able to give.

ELEANOR ROOSEVELT

If one is joyful, it means that one is faithfully living for God, and that nothing else counts; and if one gives joy to others one is doing God's work. With joy without and joy within, all is well.

JANET ERSKINE STUART

Your love has given me much joy and comfort...for your kindness has often refreshed the hearts of God's people.

PHILEMON 1:7 NLT

When hands reach out in friendship, hearts are touched with joy.

........................................................................................

........................................................................................

........................................................................................

........................................................................................

........................................................................................

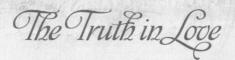

# The Truth in Love

Love is patient, love is kind. It does not envy, it does not boast,
it is not proud. It does not dishonor others, it is not self-seeking,
it is not easily angered, it keeps no record of wrongs. Love...
rejoices with the truth. It always protects, always trusts,
always hopes, always perseveres.

1 Corinthians 13:4–7 niv

Love. No greater theme can be emphasized. No stronger message
can be proclaimed. No finer song can be sung.
No better truth can be imagined.

Charles Swindoll

I wish you peace—in the world in which you live and in the
smallest corner of the heart where truth is kept. I wish you faith—
to help define your living and your life. More I cannot wish you—
except perhaps love—to make all the rest worthwhile.

Robert A. Ward

The deepest truth blooms only from the deepest love.

Heinrich Heine

.....................................................................................................................

.....................................................................................................................

.....................................................................................................................

.....................................................................................................................

# To Live, Laugh, and Love

Whole-hearted, ready laughter heals, encourages, relaxes anyone
within hearing distance. The laughter that springs from love makes
wide the space around—gives room for the loved one to enter in.

EUGENIA PRICE

If you can learn to laugh in spite of the circumstances
that surround you, you will enrich others, enrich yourself,
and more than that, you will last!

BARBARA JOHNSON

The best laughter, the laughter that can heal, the laughter
that has the truest ring, is the laughter that flowers
out of a love for life and its Giver.

MAXINE HANCOCK

Let all those who seek You rejoice and be glad in You.

PSALM 40:16 NKJV

A good laugh is as good as a prayer sometimes.

LUCY MAUD MONTGOMERY

# A Quiet Time

Open wide the windows of our spirits and fill us full of light;
open wide the door of our hearts that we may receive and
entertain You with all the powers of our adoration.

CHRISTINA ROSSETTI

We need quiet time to examine our lives openly and honestly....
Spending quiet time alone gives your mind an opportunity
to renew itself and create order.

SUSAN L. TAYLOR

Let us give all that lies within us...to pure praise, to pure
loving adoration, and to worship from a grateful heart—
a heart that is trained to look up.

AMY CARMICHAEL

Devote yourselves to prayer, being watchful and thankful.

COLOSSIANS 4:2 NIV

I am convinced beyond a shadow of any doubt that the most
valuable pursuit we can embark upon is to know God.

KAY ARTHUR

# Best Job in the World

Though motherhood is the most important of all the professions—requiring more knowledge than any other department in human affairs—there was no attention given to preparation for this office.

ELIZABETH CADY STANTON

The most important thing she'd learned over the years was that there was no way to be a perfect mother and a million ways to be a good one.

JILL CHURCHILL

May our Lord Jesus Christ himself and God our Father... encourage your hearts and strengthen you in every good deed and word.

2 THESSALONIANS 2:16–17 NIV

As a mother, my job is to take care of what is possible and trust God with the impossible.

RUTH BELL GRAHAM

........................................................................................

........................................................................................

........................................................................................

........................................................................................

........................................................................................

# We're Blessed to Bless

Not everyone possesses boundless energy or a conspicuous talent.
We are not equally blessed with great intellect or
physical beauty or emotional strength. But we have all
been given the same ability to be faithful.

GIGI GRAHAM TCHIVIDJIAN

Do all the good you can
By all the means you can
In all the ways you can
In all the places you can
To all the people you can
As long as ever you can.

JOHN WESLEY

Have a purpose in life, and having it, throw into your work
such strength of mind and muscle as God has given you.

THOMAS CARLYLE

Whatever you do, whether in word or deed,
do it all in the name of the Lord Jesus.

COLOSSIANS 3:17 NIV

.................................................................................................................

.................................................................................................................

.................................................................................................................

.................................................................................................................

# The Simplicity of Childhood

It is the little things that count
And give a mother pleasure—
The things her children bring to her
Which they so richly treasure...
The picture that is smudged a bit
With tiny fingerprints,
The colored rock, the lightning bugs,
The sticky peppermints;
The ragged, bright bouquet of flowers
A child brings, roots and all—
These things delight a mother's heart
Although they seem quite small.
A mother can see beauty
In the very smallest thing
For there's a little bit of heaven
In a small child's offering.

KATHERINE NELSON DAVIS

"Unless you accept God's kingdom in the simplicity of a child,
you'll never get in." Then...he laid his hands of blessing on them.

MARK 10:15–16 MSG

# All Creation Sings

It is an extraordinary and beautiful thing that God,
in creation...works with the beauty of matter; the reality
of things; the discoveries of the senses, all five of them;
so that we, in turn, may hear the grass growing;
see a face springing to life in love and laughter....
The offerings of creation...our glimpses of truth.

MADELEINE L'ENGLE

Whatever is good and perfect comes down to us from God
our Father, who created all the lights in the heavens.... And we,
out of all creation, became his prized possession.

JAMES 1:17–18 NLT

In all ranks of life the human heart yearns for the beautiful, and
the beautiful things that God makes are His gift to all alike.

HARRIET BEECHER STOWE

# Cherished Moments

To receive a gift, molded from love and sacrifice,
selected with care and tied up with all the excitement the
giver has to offer, is indeed rare. They don't come along often,
but when they do, cherish them.

ERMA BOMBECK

If we celebrate the years behind us
they become stepping-stones of strength and
joy for the years ahead.

Thank You, Jesus, for this day,
For my food, and for my play.
Now my evening thanks I bring
For my home and everything.
Bless me as I sleep this night,
Wake me with the morning light.

MARIE C. TURK

Rejoice always, pray continually,
give thanks in all circumstances.

1 THESSALONIANS 5:16–18 NIV

..............................................................................................

..............................................................................................

..............................................................................................

..............................................................................................

# Promises in the Present

Women of adventure have conquered their fates and
know how to live exciting and fulfilling lives right
where they are. They have learned to reinvent themselves
and find creative ways to enjoy the world and their place in it.
They know how to take mini-vacations, stop and
smell the roses, and live fully in the moment.

BARBARA JENKINS

I have learned to be content whatever the circumstances.
I know what it is to be in need, and I know what
it is to have plenty.... I can do all this through him
who gives me strength.

PHILIPPIANS 4:11–13 NIV

Normal day, let me be aware of the treasure you are.
Let me learn from you, love you, bless you before you depart.
Let me not pass you by in quest of some rare
and perfect tomorrow.

..................................................................................................

..................................................................................................

..................................................................................................

..................................................................................................

..................................................................................................

..................................................................................................

# What Children Want

Children will not remember you for the material things you provided, but for the feeling that you cherished them.

GAIL GRENIER SWEET

She is their earth.... She is their food and their bed and the extra blanket when it grows cold in the night; she is their warmth and their health and their shelter.

KATHERINE BUTLER HATHAWAY

They might not need me; but they might.
I'll let my head be just in sight;
A smile as small as mine might be
Precisely their necessity.

EMILY DICKINSON

I've cultivated a quiet heart.
Like a baby content in its mother's arms.

PSALM 131:2 MSG

# His Promised Attention

The God who created, names, and numbers the stars in the heavens also numbers the hairs of my head.... He pays attention to very big things and to very small ones. What matters to me matters to Him, and that changes my life.

God is every moment totally aware of each one of us. Totally aware in intense concentration and love.... No one passes through any area of life, happy or tragic, without the attention of God.

EUGENIA PRICE

Steep your life in God-reality, God-initiative, God-provisions. Don't worry about missing out. You'll find all your everyday human concerns will be met.

MATTHEW 6:33 MSG

We have been in God's thought from all eternity, and in His creative love, His attention never leaves us.

MICHAEL QUOIST

.................................................................................................

.................................................................................................

.................................................................................................

.................................................................................................

# The Heritage of Children

Every material goal, even if it is met, will pass away.
But the heritage of children is timeless. Our children are
our messages to the future.

BILLY GRAHAM

Creating a family in this turbulent world is an act of faith,
a wager that against all odds there will be a future,
that love can last, that the heart can triumph against all adversities
and even against the grinding wheel of time.

DEAN KOONTZ

Children are a heritage from the LORD,
offspring a reward from him.

PSALM 127:3 NIV

If our children are blank pages upon which we write their future,
then we must carefully consider what we want to write.

PATRICIA H. RUSHFORD

In every child is planted the seed of a great future.

.................................................................................................

.................................................................................................

.................................................................................................

.................................................................................................

# God's Amazing Love

Before anything else, above all else, beyond everything else,
God loves us. God loves us extravagantly, ridiculously, without
limit or condition. God is in love with us...God yearns for us.

ROBERTA BONDI

Blessed be the God and Father of our Lord Jesus Christ,
the Father of mercies and God of all comfort, who comforts us
in all our tribulation, that we may be able to comfort those
who are in any trouble, with the comfort with which we
ourselves are comforted by God.

2 CORINTHIANS 1:3–4 NKJV

The treasure our heart searches for is found
in the ocean of God's love.

JANET L. SMITH

Stand outside this evening. Look at the stars.
Know that you are special and loved
by the One who created them.

..........................................................................................................

..........................................................................................................

..........................................................................................................

..........................................................................................................

..........................................................................................................

# Mother and Child

There is no other closeness in human life like the closeness
between a mother and her baby—chronologically, physically,
and spiritually they are just a few heartbeats away
from being the same person.

SUSAN CHEVER

She speaks with wisdom,
and faithful instruction is on her tongue....
Her children arise and call her blessed.

PROVERBS 31:26, 28 NIV

There is an enduring tenderness in the love of a mother to a
[child] that transcends all other affections of the heart.

WASHINGTON IRVING

No joy in nature is so sublimely affecting as the joy of a
mother at the good fortune of her child.

JEAN PAUL RICHTER

A mother's arms are made of tenderness and children
sleep soundly in them.

VICTOR HUGO

# Promised Dividends

Choices can change our lives profoundly. The choice to mend
a broken relationship, to say yes to a difficult assignment,
to lay aside some important work to play with a child,
to visit some forgotten person—these small choices
may affect our lives eternally.

GLORIA GAITHER

We must not, in trying to think about how we can
make a big difference, ignore the small daily differences
we can make which, over time, add up to big differences
that we often cannot foresee.

MARIAN WRIGHT EDELMAN

Let your light shine before others, that they may see your
good deeds and glorify your Father in heaven.

MATTHEW 5:16 NIV

Invest in people rather than things for
herein lies eternal dividends.

....................................................................................................

....................................................................................................

....................................................................................................

....................................................................................................

....................................................................................................

# A Mother's Influence

The blossom cannot tell what becomes of its fragrance as it drifts away, just as no person can tell what becomes of her influence as she continues through life.

The fullness of our heart is expressed in our eyes, in our touch, in what we write, in what we say, in the way we walk, the way we receive, the way we need.

MOTHER TERESA

A child's hand in yours—what tenderness and power it arouses. You are instantly the very touchstone of wisdom and strength.

MARJORIE HOLMES

Train up a child in the way he should go,
And when he is old he will not depart from it.

PROVERBS 22:6 NKJV

A mother is not a person to lean on, but a person to make leaning unnecessary.

DOROTHY CANFIELD FISHER

........................................................................

........................................................................

........................................................................

........................................................................

# The World of Wonder

A fiery sunset, tiny pansies by the wayside, the sound
of raindrops tapping on the roof—what extraordinary delight
we find in the simple wonders of life! With wide eyes and
full hearts, we may cherish what others often miss.

What a wildly wonderful world, GOD! You made it all,
with Wisdom at your side, made earth overflow
with your wonderful creations.

PSALM 104:24 MSG

There are no seven wonders of the world in the eyes of a child.
There are seven million.

WALT STREIGHTIFF

Loving Creator, help me reawaken my childlike
sense of wonder at the delights of Your world!

MARILYN MORGAN HELLEBERG

...........................................................................................................................

...........................................................................................................................

...........................................................................................................................

...........................................................................................................................

...........................................................................................................................

...........................................................................................................................

# The Promise of Faith

If it can be verified, we don't need faith.... Faith is
for that which lies on the other side of reason. Faith is what
makes life bearable, with all its tragedies and ambiguities
and sudden, startling joys.

MADELEINE L'ENGLE

True faith drops its letter in the post office box and lets it go.
Distrust holds on to a corner of it and wonders that
the answer never comes.

L. B. COWMAN

Finding acceptance with joy, whatever the circumstances of life—
whether they are petty annoyances or fiery trials—
this is a living faith that grows.

MARY LOU STEIGLEDER

I pray that out of his glorious riches he may strengthen you with
power through his Spirit in your inner being, so that Christ
may dwell in your hearts through faith.

EPHESIANS 3:16–17 NIV

# Wonderful Peace

May your footsteps set you upon a lifetime journey of love.
May you wake each day with His blessings and sleep each night in
His keeping. And may you always walk in His tender care.

O heavenly Father, protect and bless all things that have breath:
guard them from all evil and let them sleep in peace.

ALBERT SCHWEITZER

Only God gives true peace—a quiet gift He sets within us just
when we think we've exhausted our search for it.

May God kiss you with His peace,
as a mother kisses her little child.
And may you know that peace isn't
a pot of gold rewarded to you
after chasing some rainbow's end—
it's a gift.

Grace and peace to you from God our Father
and from the Lord Jesus Christ.

ROMANS 1:7 NIV

.........................................................................................................

.........................................................................................................

.........................................................................................................

.........................................................................................................

# God Bless Your Children

Remember you are very special to God as His precious child.
He has promised to complete the good work He
has begun in you. As you continue to grow in Him,
He will teach you to be a blessing to others.

GARY SMALLEY AND JOHN TRENT

Just as Jesus took the children, put His hands on them
and blessed them...we can hold our children in our arms,
touching, blessing, and praying over them.

QUIN SHERRER

Bless our children, God, and help us so to
fashion their souls by precept and example
that they may ever...honor Your name.

UNION PRAYER BOOK

May the LORD richly bless both you and your children.

PSALM 115:14 NLT

# Special Gifts We Share

Our greatest responsibility today may be
the unselfish sacrifice of our time, talent, and love in the
lives of those little ones around us.

SUSAN DOWNS

Each one of us is God's special work of art. Through us,
He teaches and inspires, delights and encourages,
informs and uplifts all those who view our lives.

JONI EARECKSON TADA

Give, and it will be given to you. A good measure, pressed down,
shaken together and running over, will be poured into your lap.
For with the measure you use, it will be measured to you.

LUKE 6:38 NIV

God gave me my gifts. I will do all I can to
show Him how grateful I am to Him.

GRACE LIVINGSTON HILL

.....................................................................................................

.....................................................................................................

.....................................................................................................

.....................................................................................................

.....................................................................................................

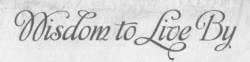

# Wisdom to Live By

At the end of your life you will never regret not
having passed one more test, not winning one more verdict,
or not closing one more deal. You will regret time not spent
with a husband, a friend, a child, or a parent.

BARBARA BUSH

Whenever I need help being a mother, I remember my mother
and grandmother, women who planted seeds of wisdom in my
soul, like a secret garden, to flower even in the bitterest cold.

JUDITH TOWSE-ROBERTS

Wisdom is knowing the truth and telling it in love.

It is always wise to stop wishing for things long enough
to enjoy the fragrance of those now flowering.

PATRICE GIFFORD

Teach us to number our days,
that we may gain a heart of wisdom.

PSALM 90:12 NIV

# Irreplaceable

All that we have and are is one of the unique and never-to-be repeated ways God has chosen to express Himself in space and time. Each of us, made in His image and likeness, is yet another promise He has made to the universe that He will continue to love it and care for it.

BRENNAN MANNING

If God gives such attention to the appearance of wildflowers—most of which are never even seen—don't you think he'll attend to you, take pride in you, do his best for you?

MATTHEW 6:30 MSG

We have missed the full impact of the Gospel if we have not discovered what it is to be ourselves, loved by God, irreplaceable in His sight, unique among our fellow men.

BRUCE LARSON

Embrace your uniqueness. Time is much too short to be living someone else's life.

KOBI YAMADA

# A Reason for Praise

I have never committed the least matter to God,
that I have not had reason for infinite praise.

ANNA SHIPTON

How much of our lives are...well...so daily. How often
our hours are filled with the mundane, seemingly unimportant
things that have to be done, whether at home or work.
These very "daily" tasks could become a celebration of praise.
"It is through consecration," someone has said,
"that drudgery is made divine."

GIGI GRAHAM TCHIVIDJIAN

Then we your people, the sheep of your pasture,
will thank you forever and ever,
praising your greatness from generation to generation.

PSALM 79:13 NLT

They that trust the Lord find many things to praise Him for.
Praise follows trust.

LILY MAY GOULD

...........................................................................................................................

...........................................................................................................................

...........................................................................................................................

...........................................................................................................................

# Eternal Moments

Friendships, family ties, the companionship of little children,
an autumn forest flung in prodigality against a deep blue sky,
the intricate design and haunting fragrance of a flower,
the counterpoint of a Bach fugue or the melodic line of a
Beethoven sonata, the fluted note of bird song,
the glowing glory of a sunset: the world is aflame
with things of eternal moment.

E. MARGARET CLARKSON

Life is what we are alive to. It is not length but breadth....
Be alive to...goodness, kindness, purity, love, history,
poetry, music, flowers, stars, God, and eternal hope.

MALTBIE D. BABCOCK

You make known to me the path of life;
you will fill me with joy in your presence,
with eternal pleasures at your right hand.

PSALM 16:11 NIV

........................................................................................

........................................................................................

........................................................................................

........................................................................................

........................................................................................

........................................................................................

# A Mother's Own Gift

Oh God, You have given me...a life of clay.
Put Your big hands around mine and guide my hands
so that every time I make a mark on this life, it will be Your mark.

GLORIA GAITHER

If you...know how to give good gifts to your children,
how much more will your Father in heaven
give good gifts to those who ask him!

MATTHEW 7:11 NIV

Maybe all I could do was mother.... And yet, why did I
feel so fulfilled when I bedded down three kids
between clean sheets? What if raising and instilling values
in three children and turning them into worthwhile
human beings would be the most important contribution
I ever made in my lifetime?

ERMA BOMBECK

Life, love, and laughter—
what priceless gifts to give our children.

PHYLLIS CAMPBELL DRYDEN

.......................................................................................................................

.......................................................................................................................

.......................................................................................................................

.......................................................................................................................

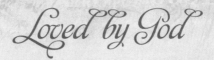

# Loved by God

We think God's love rises and falls
with our performance. It doesn't.... He loves you for
whose you are: you are His child.

MAX LUCADO

For God so loved the world that He gave His only
begotten Son, that whoever believes in Him
should not perish but have everlasting life.

JOHN 3:16 NKJV

Our greatness rests solely on the fact that God in His
incomprehensible goodness has bestowed His love upon us.
God does not love us because we are so valuable;
we are valuable because God loves us.

HELMUT THIELICKE

The Creator thinks enough of you to have sent Someone
very special so that you might have life—
abundantly, joyfully, completely, and victoriously.

# A Child's Worldview

The most successful parents are those who have
the skill to get behind the eyes of a child, seeing what they see,
thinking what they think, feeling what they feel.

JAMES DOBSON

If children are to keep their inborn sense of wonder...
they need the companionship of at least one adult who
can share it, rediscovering with them the joy, excitement,
and mystery of the world we live in.

RACHEL CARSON

Keep your eyes open for GOD, watch for his works;
be alert for signs of his presence.
Remember the world of wonders he has made.

PSALM 105:4–5 MSG

It is a special gift to be able to view the world
through the eyes of a child.

.......................................................................................................

.......................................................................................................

.......................................................................................................

.......................................................................................................

.......................................................................................................

.......................................................................................................

# A Mother's Heart

Love grows from our capacity to give what is deepest
within ourselves and also receive what is the deepest within
another person. The heart becomes an ocean strong and deep,
launching all on its tide.

My mother and I have laughed over nothing and cried
over everything. We understand each other's fears, losses, and
sense of humor. She holds my heart like no one else can.

JANETTE OKE

Being a full-time mother is one of the highest-salaried jobs
in any field since the payment is pure love.

MILDRED B. VERMONT

You gave me life and showed me your unfailing love.
My life was preserved by your care.

JOB 10:12 NLT

A mother's love is the heart of the home. Her children's
sense of security and self-worth are found there.

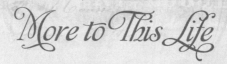

# More to This Life

God desires that the work we do bring us enduring joy
and satisfaction. This will naturally happen when our efforts are
labors of love that bring Him glory and praise.

<small>BEVERLY LaHAYE</small>

Why is everyone hungry for more?
"More, more," they say. "More, more."
I have God's more-than-enough,
More joy in one ordinary day
Than they get in all their shopping sprees.
At day's end I'm ready for sound sleep,
For you, God, have put my life back together.

<small>PSALM 4:6–8 MSG</small>

If there is a God who speaks anywhere, surely He speaks here:
through waking up and working, through going away
and coming back again, through people you read and books
you meet, through falling asleep in the dark.

<small>FREDERICK BUECHNER</small>

# Everyday Miracles

I think miracles exist in part as gifts and in part as clues that
there is something beyond the flat world we see.

PEGGY NOONAN

The child must know that he is a miracle, that since
the beginning of the world there hasn't been,
and until the end of the world there will not be,
another child like him.

PABLO CASALS

Come and see what our God has done,
what awesome miracles he performs.

PSALM 66:5 NLT

The miracles of nature do not seem miracles because they
are so common. If no one had ever seen a flower, even a dandelion
would be the most startling event in the world.

Know that you yourself are a miracle.

NORMAN VINCENT PEALE

........................................................................................

........................................................................................

........................................................................................

........................................................................................

# Encouragement Is...

Encouragement is being a good listener,
being positive, letting others know you accept them for
who they are. It is offering hope, caring about
the feelings of another, understanding.

GIGI GRAHAM TCHIVIDJIAN

A mother is one who knows you as you really are,
understands where you've been, accepts who
you've become, and still gently invites you to grow.

A word of encouragement to those we meet,
a cheerful smile in the supermarket, a card or
letter to a friend, a readiness to witness when opportunity
is given—all are practical ways in which
we may let His light shine through us.

ELIZABETH B. JONES

Encourage each other, be of one mind, live in peace.
And the God of love and peace will be with you.

2 CORINTHIANS 13:11 NIV

........................................................................................................

........................................................................................................

........................................................................................................

........................................................................................................

# Joys of Motherhood

Sense of humor; God's great gift
causes spirits to uplift,
Helps to make our bodies mend;
lightens burdens; cheers a friend;
Tickles children; elders grin
at this warmth that glows within;
Surely in the great hereafter
heaven must be full of laughter!

Now, as always, the most automated appliance
in a household is the mother.

BEVERLY JONES

Children seldom misquote you. They more often repeat
word for word what you shouldn't have said.

MAE MALOO

A twinkle in the eye means joy in the heart.

PROVERBS 15:30 MSG

.................................................................................

.................................................................................

.................................................................................

.................................................................................

.................................................................................

# God Loves Our Children

For my dear little child I'd lasso the moon
and give you my love on a silver spoon.
I'd run 'round the world and back again, too,
to grant you the hope of days bright and new.
But all that I have and all that I do
is nothing compared to God's love for you.

Children of the heavenly Father
Safely in His bosom gather;
Nestling bird nor star in heaven
Such a refuge e'er was given.

LINA SANDELL BERG

See what great love the Father has lavished on us,
that we should be called children of God!
And that is what we are!

1 JOHN 3:1 NIV

After the love of God, a mother's affection is
the greatest treasure here below.

........................................................................................

........................................................................................

........................................................................................

........................................................................................

# The Richness of Friendship

We are so very rich if we know just a few people
in a way in which we know no others.

CATHERINE BRAMWELL BOOTH

Knowing what to say is not always necessary;
just the presence of a caring friend can
make a world of difference.

SHERI CURRY

Stay true to the Lord. I love you and long to see you,
dear friends, for you are my joy.

PHILIPPIANS 4:1 NLT

I am only as strong as the coffee I drink,
the hairspray I use, and the friends I have.

A friend understands what you are trying to say...
even when your thoughts aren't fitting into words.

ANN D. PARRISH

# Homegrown Happiness

How necessary it is to cultivate a spirit of joy. It is a
psychological truth that the physical acts of reverence and
devotion make one feel devout. The courteous gesture
increases one's respect for others. To act lovingly is to
begin to feel loving, and certainly to act joyfully brings joy
to others which in turn makes one feel joyful.
I believe we are called to the duty of delight.

DOROTHY DAY

Sometimes the laughter in mothering is the
recognition of the ironies and absurdities. Sometime, though,
it's just pure, unthinking delight.

BARBARA SCHAPIRO

Happy are those who hear the joyful call to worship,
for they will walk in the light of your presence, LORD.

PSALM 89:15 NLT

To be able to find joy in another's joy,
that is the secret of happiness.

......................................................................................................

......................................................................................................

......................................................................................................

......................................................................................................

# A Covering of Prayer

When you were small
And just a touch away,
I covered you with blankets
Against the cool night air.
But now that you are tall
And out of reach,
I fold my hands
And cover you with prayer.

DONA MADDUX COOPER

Lord, thank You for my children. Please inspire me with
ways to show them my love and Yours. I want them
to feel appreciated. I want to help and encourage them....
I want to bless them.

QUIN SHERRER

I have not stopped giving thanks for you,
remembering you in my prayers.

EPHESIANS 1:16 NIV

# A Mother's Love

A Mother's love is something
that no one can explain,
It is made of deep devotion
and of sacrifice and pain....
It believes beyond believing
when the world around condemns,
And it glows with all the beauty
of the rarest, brightest gems.

HELEN STEINER RICE


A mother is someone who dreams great dreams for you,
but then she lets you chase the dreams you have
for yourself and loves you just the same. In the end,
she believes in your dreams as much as you do.


Finally, all of you should be in agreement, understanding
each other, loving each other as family, being kind and humble.

1 PETER 3:8 NCV


If there be one thing pure...that can endure,
when all else passes away...it is a mother's love.

MARCHIONESS DE SPADARA

# Promises of the Day

Not every day of our lives is overflowing with
joy and celebration. But there are moments
when our hearts nearly burst within us for the sheer joy
of being alive. The first sight of our newborn babies, the warmth
of love in another's eyes, the fresh scent of rain
on a hot summer's eve—moments like these renew in us
a heartfelt appreciation for life.

GWEN ELLIS

Experience God in the breathless wonder
and startling beauty that is all around you.
His sun shines warm upon your face.
His wind whispers in the treetops. Like the first
rays of morning light, celebrate the start
of each day with God.

You will show us your faithfulness and
unfailing love as you promised.

MICAH 7:20 NLT

......................................................................................................

......................................................................................................

......................................................................................................

......................................................................................................

......................................................................................................

# My Heart Is Content

A wise gardener plants his seeds, then has the good sense
not to dig them up every few days to see if a crop is on the way.
Likewise, we must be patient as God brings the answers...
in His own good time.

QUIN SHERRER

Where the soul is full of peace and joy,
outward surroundings and circumstances
are of comparatively little account.

HANNAH WHITALL SMITH

Everything has its wonders, even darkness and silence,
and I learn, whatever state I may be in, therein to be content.

HELEN KELLER

If you're content to simply be yourself,
your life will count for plenty.

MATTHEW 23:11 MSG

# The Blessing of Gratitude

Gratitude unlocks the fullness of life. It turns
what we have into enough, and more....
It can turn a meal into a feast, a house into a home,
a stranger into a friend. Gratitude makes sense
of our past, brings peace for today,
and creates a vision for tomorrow.

MELODY BEATTIE

Be thankful. Let the message of Christ dwell among you richly
as you teach and admonish one another with all wisdom
through psalms, hymns, and songs from the Spirit,
singing to God with gratitude in your hearts.

COLOSSIANS 3:15–16 NIV

Were there no God we would be in this glorious world
with grateful hearts and no one to thank.

CHRISTINA ROSSETTI

Gratitude is the memory of the heart.

LYDIA MARIA CHILD

# Family Ties

We were a strange little band of characters, trudging
through life sharing diseases and toothpaste, coveting one
another's desserts, hiding shampoo, borrowing money,
locking each other out of our rooms, inflicting pain
and kissing to heal it in the same instant, loving, laughing,
defending, and trying to figure out the common thread
that bound us all together.

ERMA BOMBECK

A family is a group of individuals who are related
to one another by marriage, birth, or adoption—
nothing more, nothing else. This is not merely human in origin.
It is God's marvelous creation.

JAMES DOBSON

Other things may change us, but we start and end with family.

ANTHONY BRANDT

Love each other with genuine affection,
and take delight in honoring each other.

ROMANS 12:10 NLT

............................................................................................................

............................................................................................................

............................................................................................................

............................................................................................................

# Taking Time to Love

Dear Lord, please help me to remember
to take the time to bestow the kisses today
that I want loved ones to remember tomorrow.

JENNIFER THOMAS

Getting things accomplished isn't nearly as
important as taking time for love.

JANETTE OKE

Take time to notice all the usually unnoticed, simple things in life.
Delight in the never-ending hope that's available every day!

WENDY MOORE

Time is a very precious gift of God; so precious
that it's only given to us moment by moment.

AMELIA BARR

Love each other as if your life depended on it.
Love makes up for practically anything.

1 PETER 4:8 MSG

# The Blessing of Dreams

It is necessary that we dream now and then. No one ever
achieved anything from the smallest to the greatest
unless the dream was dreamed first.

LAURA INGALLS WILDER

When you are inspired by a dream, God has hit
the ball into your court. Now you have to
hit it back with commitment.

ROBERT SCHULLER

Now to him who is able to do immeasurably more
than all we ask or imagine, according to his power that is
at work within us, to him be glory.

EPHESIANS 3:20–21 NIV

Do not pray for dreams equal to your powers.
Pray for powers equal to your dreams.

ADELAIDE ANN PROCTER

We need time to dream, time to remember,
and time to reach the infinite. Time to be.

GLADYS TABER

..............................................................................................

..............................................................................................

..............................................................................................

# Moms Bring Out the Best

Women can do no greater thing than to create
the climate of love in their homes.... Real love strengthens and
matures and leaves the loved one free to grow.

EUGENIA PRICE

Listening...means taking a vigorous, human interest
in what is being told us. You can listen like a blank wall
or like a splendid auditorium where every sound
comes back fuller and richer.

ALICE DUER MILLER

Mama's order was heavenly. It had to do
with thoroughness...and taking plenty of time.
It had to do with taking plenty of time with me.

SUZANNAH LESSARD

Make the most of every opportunity.
Be gracious in your speech. The goal is
to bring out the best in others.

COLOSSIANS 4:5 MSG

........................................................................................................

........................................................................................................

........................................................................................................

........................................................................................................

# Thank You, Lord!

Our thanksgiving today should include those things
which we take for granted, and we should continually praise
our God, who is true to His promise, who has provided
and retained the necessities for our living.

BETTY FUHRMAN

Thank God for dirty dishes;
They have a tale to tell.
While other folks go hungry,
We're eating pretty well.
With home, and health, and happiness,
We shouldn't want to fuss;
For by this stack of evidence,
God's very good to us.

Give thanks in all circumstances; for this is
God's will for you in Christ Jesus.

1 THESSALONIANS 5:18 NIV

# One of a Kind

Everyone has a unique role to fill in the world
and is important in some respect. Everyone, including
and perhaps especially you, is indispensable.

Heavenly Father, thank You for the unique personalities
that You have given to each and every child. Help me
to discover each talent and gift with which You have blessed
my children, and may I learn how to best cultivate each of the
blossoms You have planted within their souls. Amen.

KIM BOYCE

Though two children have the same parents,
the same values, the same everything, they turn out different.
Isn't that the genius of God?

In his grace, God has given us
different gifts for doing certain things well.

ROMANS 12:6 NLT

........................................................................................

........................................................................................

........................................................................................

........................................................................................

........................................................................................

# Love All Around

There is no need to plead that the love of God
shall fill our hearts as though He were unwilling to fill us....
Love is pressing around us on all sides like air.
Cease to resist it and instantly love takes possession.

AMY CARMICHAEL

Nothing can separate you from His love,
absolutely nothing.... God is enough for time,
and God is enough for eternity. God is enough!

HANNAH WHITALL SMITH

The most important commandment is this:...
"Love the LORD your God with all your heart,
all your soul, all your mind, and all your strength."
The second is equally important:
"Love your neighbor as yourself."

MARK 12:29–31 NLT

Open your hearts to the love God instills....
God loves you tenderly. What He gives you is not to be
kept under lock and key, but to be shared.

...........................................................................................................................

...........................................................................................................................

...........................................................................................................................

...........................................................................................................................

# A Guiding Hand

I'll show my children right from wrong,
encourage dreams and hope;
explain respect for others,
while teaching them to cope
with outside pressures, inside fears,
a world that's less than whole;
and through it all I'll nurture
my children's most precious soul!
Though oftentimes a struggle,
this job I'll never trade;
for in my hand tomorrow lives...
a future God has made.

Teach your children why you believe what you believe.
Don't ask them to accept your beliefs blindly.... Teach them
to think for themselves. God's Word can withstand the test.

PAUL MEIER

Children, come and listen to me.
I will teach you to worship the LORD.

PSALM 34:11 NCV

# In God's Care

There will be days which are great and everything
goes as planned. There will be other days when
we aren't sure why we got out of bed. Regardless
of which kind of day it is, we can be assured
that God takes care of our daily needs.

EMILIE BARNES

Be still, and in the quiet moments, listen to the voice
of your heavenly Father. His words can renew your spirit...
no one knows you and your needs like He does.

JANET L. SMITH

If you have a special need today, focus your
full attention on the goodness and greatness of your Father
rather than on the size of your need. Your need is so small
compared to His ability to meet it.

[God] takes care of everyone in time of need.
His love never quits.

PSALM 136:25 MSG

.................................................................................................

.................................................................................................

.................................................................................................

.................................................................................................

# I Believe

Within each of us there is an inner place
where the living God Himself longs to dwell,
our sacred center of belief.

Faith is not an effort, a striving, a ceaseless seeking,
as so many earnest souls suppose, but rather a letting go,
an abandonment, an abiding rest in God that nothing,
not even the soul's shortcomings, can disturb.

Let your roots grow down into him, and let your lives
be built on him. Then your faith will grow strong
in the truth you were taught, and you
will overflow with thankfulness.

COLOSSIANS 2:7 NLT

Faith allows us to continually delight in life since
we have placed our needs in God's hands.

JANET L. SMITH

Faith sees the invisible, believes the incredible,
and receives the impossible.

........................................................................................................

........................................................................................................

........................................................................................................

........................................................................................................

# My Mother, My Friend

Oh, the comfort, the inexpressible comfort of feeling safe
with a person—having neither to weigh thoughts nor
measure words, but pouring them all right out just as they are,
chaff and grain together, certain that a faithful hand
will take and sift them, keep what is worth keeping and then,
with the breath of kindness, blow the rest away.

DINAH MARIA MULOCK CRAIK

Having someone who understands is a great
blessing for ourselves. Being someone who understands
is a great blessing to others.

JANETTE OKE

The fruit of the Spirit is love, joy, peace, forbearance, kindness,
goodness, faithfulness, gentleness and self-control.

GALATIANS 5:22–23 NIV

We should all have one person who
knows how to bless us despite the evidence.

PHYLLIS THEROUX

.....................................................................................................................

.....................................................................................................................

.....................................................................................................................

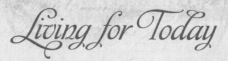

# Living for Today

What we feel, think, and do this moment influences
both our present and the future in ways we may never know.
Begin. Start right where you are. Consider
your possibilities and find inspiration...to add
more meaning and zest to your life.

ALEXANDRA STODDARD

Live for today but hold your hands open to tomorrow.
Anticipate the future and its changes with joy.
There is a seed of God's love in every event,
every circumstance, every...situation in which
you may find yourself.

BARBARA JOHNSON

Forgetting what is behind and straining toward what is ahead,
I press on toward the goal to win the prize for which
God has called me heavenward in Christ Jesus.

PHILIPPIANS 3:13–14 NIV

......................................................................................

......................................................................................

......................................................................................

......................................................................................

......................................................................................

......................................................................................

# God Bless You

Lift up your eyes.

Your heavenly Father waits to bless you—
in inconceivable ways to make your life
what you never dreamed it could be.

ANNE ORTLUND

No one can fully measure the blessings that come
to the life of the one who has a praying mother.

ROY LESSIN

I thank God, my mother,
for the blessing you are...
for the joy of your laughter...
the comfort of your prayers...
the warmth of your smile.

May the LORD, the God of your ancestors, increase you
a thousand times and bless you as he has promised!

DEUTERONOMY 1:11 NIV

............................................................................................

............................................................................................

............................................................................................

............................................................................................

............................................................................................

# Heart Full of Joy

Our hearts were made for joy. Our hearts were made to
enjoy the One who created them. Too deeply planted
to be much affected by the ups and downs of life,
this joy is a knowing and a being known by our Creator.
He sets our hearts alight with radiant joy.

WENDY MOORE

God knows everything about us.... And He loves us!
Surely this is enough to open the wellsprings of joy....
And joy is always a source of strength.

HANNAH WHITALL SMITH

That I am here is a wonderful mystery
to which I will respond with joy.

All who seek the LORD will praise him.
Their hearts will rejoice with everlasting joy.

PSALM 22:26 NLT

.........................................................................................

.........................................................................................

.........................................................................................

.........................................................................................

.........................................................................................

# Light for the Way

God has not promised skies always blue,
flower-strewn pathways all our lives through;
God has not promised sun without rain,
joy without sorrow, peace without pain.
But God has promised strength for the day,
rest for the labor, light for the way,
grace for the trials, help from above,
unfailing sympathy, undying love.

ANNIE JOHNSON FLINT

Faith in small things has repercussions
that ripple all the way out. In a huge, dark room
a little match can light up the place.

JONI EARECKSON TADA

I believe that God is in me as the sun is in the color
and fragrance of a flower—the Light in my darkness,
the Voice in my silence.

HELEN KELLER

Your word is a lamp for my feet, and a light on my path.

PSALM 119:105 NIV

# My Strength

God's love is like a river springing up in the Divine Substance and flowing endlessly through His creation, filling all things with life and goodness and strength.

THOMAS MERTON


Should we feel at times disheartened and discouraged, a simple movement of heart toward God will renew our powers. Whatever He may demand of us, He will give us at the moment the strength and courage that we need.

FRANÇOIS FÉNELON


God never abandons anyone on whom He has set His love; nor does Christ, the good shepherd, ever lose track of His sheep.

J. I. PACKER


The LORD is my strength and my shield;
my heart trusts in him, and he helps me.

PSALM 28:7 NIV

.......................................................................................................

.......................................................................................................

.......................................................................................................

.......................................................................................................

.......................................................................................................

# The Blessing of Friendship

To have someone who wants to absorb us, who wants to
understand the shape and structure of our lives, who will listen for
more than our words, is one of friendship's greatest gifts.

PAUL D. ROBBINS

Only He who created the wonders of the world
entwines hearts in an eternal way.

The friend who is really worth having is the one
who will listen to your deepest hurts
and feel they are hers too.

Many women...have buoyed me up in times of weariness
and stress. Each friend was important.... Their words have
seasoned my life. Influence, just like salt shaken out,
is hard to see, but its flavor is hard to miss.

PAM FARREL

A friend loves at all times.

PROVERBS 17:17 NIV

...................................................................................................

...................................................................................................

...................................................................................................

...................................................................................................

# A Mother's Contentment

Let the day suffice, with all its joys and failings, its little triumphs and defeats.... Happily, if sleepily, welcome evening as a time of rest, and let it slip away, losing nothing.

KATHLEEN NORRIS

God is helping me to be content to set certain gifts on the shelf at present for the sake of my family. He is teaching me that He is more interested in what I am than in what I do.

SANDRA K. STRUBHAR

We brought nothing into the world, and we can take nothing out of it. But if we have food and clothing, we will be content with that.

1 TIMOTHY 6:7–8 NIV

Blessed is the person who is too busy to
worry in the daytime
and too sleepy to worry at night.

CAROLINE SCHROEDER

# Praise and Adoration

God is sheer being itself—Spirit. Those who worship him
must do it out of their very being, their spirits,
their true selves, in adoration.

We can go through all the activities of our days in
joyful awareness of God's presence with whispered prayers of
praise and adoration flowing continuously from our hearts.

RICHARD J. FOSTER

It is right and good that we, for all things, at all times,
and in all places, give thanks and praise to You, O God.
We worship You, we confess to You, we praise You, we bless You,
we sing to You, and we give thanks to You.

LANCELOT ANDREWES

Love wholeheartedly, be surprised, give thanks and praise—
then you will discover the fullness of your life.

DAVID STEINDL-RAST

..........................................................................................

..........................................................................................

..........................................................................................

..........................................................................................

..........................................................................................

# Extra in the Ordinary

The incredible gift of the ordinary!
Glory comes streaming from the table of daily life.

MACRINA WIEDERKEHR

See each morning a world made anew, as if it were
the morning of the very first day;...treasure and use it,
as if it were the final hour of the very last day.

FAY HARTZELL ARNOLD

God still draws near to us in the ordinary, commonplace,
everyday experiences and places.... He comes in surprising ways.

HENRY GARIEPY

Take your everyday, ordinary life—your sleeping, eating,
going-to-work, and walking-around life—and place it before God
as an offering. Embracing what God does for you is
the best thing you can do for him.

ROMANS 12:1 MSG

.................................................................................................................

.................................................................................................................

.................................................................................................................

.................................................................................................................

.................................................................................................................

.................................................................................................................

# Living in Truth

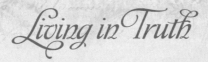

To follow truth as blind men long for light,
To do my best from dawn of day till night,
To keep my heart fit for His holy sight,
And answer when He calls.
This is my task.

MAUDE LOUISE RAY

Jesus answered, "I am the way and the truth and the life.
No one comes to the Father except through me."

JOHN 14:6 NIV

I am amazed by the sayings of Christ. They seem
truer than anything I have ever read. And they
certainly turn the world upside down.

KATHERINE BUTLER HATHAWAY

Truth is always exciting. Speak it, then.
Life is dull without it.

PEARL S. BUCK

..............................................................................................

..............................................................................................

..............................................................................................

..............................................................................................

..............................................................................................

# Blessings for the Children

There is no greater pleasure than bringing to the uncluttered,
supple mind of a child the delight of knowing God and the many
rich things He has given us to enjoy.

GLADYS M. HUNT

There are two lasting bequests we can give our children.
One of these is roots; the other, wings.

HODDING CARTER III

The LORD bless you, and keep you;
The LORD make His face shine on you,
And be gracious to you;
The LORD lift up His countenance on you,
And give you peace.

NUMBERS 6:24–26 NASB

Recognizing the good in children is one of the
greatest gifts we can give to them.

The best gift you can give a child is love.

..................................................................................................

..................................................................................................

..................................................................................................

..................................................................................................

# At Mother's Knee

Stories first heard at mother's knee are never wholly forgotten—
a little spring that never quite dries up in our journey
through scorching years.

G. Ruffini

To discipline a child produces wisdom....
Discipline your children, and they will give you peace
of mind and will make your heart glad.

Proverbs 29:15, 17 NLT

God, help me to be honest
so my children will learn honesty.
Help me to be kind
so my children will learn kindness.
Help me to be faithful
so my children will learn faith.
Help me to love
so that my children will be loving.

Marian Wright Edelman

# Little Acts of Kindness

Kindness is the only service that will stand the storm of life and not wash out. It will wear well and be remembered long after the prism of politeness or the complexion of courtesy has faded away.

Notice words of compassion. Seek out deeds of kindness. These are like the doves from heaven, pointing out to you who are the ones blessed with inner grace and beauty.

CHRISTOPHER DE VINCK

If you can help anybody even a little, be glad; up the steps of usefulness and kindness, God will lead you on to happiness and friendship.

MALTBIE D. BABCOCK

The older you get the more you realize that kindness is synonymous with happiness.

LIONEL BARRYMORE

Be kind to one another, tenderhearted, forgiving one another, even as God in Christ forgave you.

EPHESIANS 4:32 NKJV

# Through the Eyes of a Child

My child took a crayon
In her little hand
And started to draw
As if by command.

I looked on with pleasure
But couldn't foresee
What the few simple lines
Were going to be.

What are you drawing?
I asked, by and by.
I'm making a picture
Of God in the sky.

But nobody knows
What God looks like, I sighed.
They will when I'm finished
She calmly replied.

SHERWIN KAUFMAN

Jesus said, "Let the little children come to me, and do not hinder them, for the kingdom of heaven belongs to such as these."

MATTHEW 19:14 NIV

..................................................................................

..................................................................................

..................................................................................

# The Gift of Simplicity

Don't ever let yourself get so busy that you miss those little but important extras in life—the beauty of a day...the smile of a friend...the serenity of a quiet moment alone. For it is often life's smallest pleasures and gentlest joys that make the biggest and most lasting difference.

A devout life does bring wealth, but it's the rich simplicity of being yourself before God.

1 TIMOTHY 6:6 MSG

Simplicity will enable you to leap lightly. Increasingly you will find yourself living in a state of grace, finding...the sacred in the ordinary, the mystical in the mundane.

DAVID YOUNT

Walk and talk and work and laugh with your friends, but behind the scenes, keep up the life of simple prayer and inward worship.

THOMAS R. KELLY

.................................................................................

.................................................................................

.................................................................................

.................................................................................

.................................................................................

# A Mother's Thoughts

Part of the curse of motherhood is never
knowing if you're doing a good job. But part of the joy
is realizing no one's really keeping score.

Dale Hanson Bourke

More so than any other human relationship, in fact,
overwhelmingly more, motherhood means being instantly
interruptible, responsive, and responsible.

Mother had a thousand thoughts to get through within a day,
and...most of these were about avoiding disaster.

Natalie Kusz

Today's Forecast: Partly rational with brief periods of coherent
thought giving way to complete apathy by tonight.

Sherrie Weaver

Cast your cares on the LORD
and he will sustain you.

Psalm 55:22 NIV

............................................................................................

............................................................................................

............................................................................................

............................................................................................

# The Strength of Family

Family faces are magic mirrors. Looking at people who belong to us, we see the past, present, and future.

GAIL LUMET BUCKLEY

The family is a school of mutual help. Each member depends on every other.... Each helps the other when and where the help is most needed. And every word and deed of unselfish love comes back in blessings on its author.

T. L. CUYLER

You've blessed my family so that it will continue in your presence always. Because you have blessed it, GOD, it's really blessed—blessed for good!

1 CHRONICLES 17:27 MSG

Call it clan, call it a network, call it a tribe, call it a family. Whatever you call it, whoever you are, you need one.

JANE HOWARD

.................................................................................

.................................................................................

.................................................................................

.................................................................................

.................................................................................

# Close to Him

Incredible as it may seem, God wants our companionship.
He wants to have us close to Him. He wants to be a father to us,
to shield us, to protect us, to counsel us, and to guide us
in our way through life.

BILLY GRAHAM

I will let God's peace infuse every part of today. As the chaos
swirls and life's demands pull at me on all sides, I will
breathe in God's peace that surpasses all understanding.
He has promised that He would set within me
a peace too deeply planted to be affected by unexpected
or exhausting demands.

WENDY MOORE

It is good for me to draw near to God;
I have put my trust in the Lord GOD.

PSALM 73:28 NKJV

...............................................................................................

...............................................................................................

...............................................................................................

...............................................................................................

...............................................................................................

...............................................................................................

# A Generous Spirit

Love is not getting, but giving.... It is goodness and honor and peace and pure living—yes, love is that and it is the best thing in the world and the thing that lives the longest.

HENRY VAN DYKE

If your gift is to encourage others, be encouraging.
If it is giving, give generously.... Don't just pretend to love others.
Really love them.

ROMANS 12:8–9 NLT

The fountain of beauty is the heart, and every generous thought illustrates the walls of your chamber.

FRANCIS QUARLES

Giving is the secret of a healthy life...not necessarily money, but whatever one has of encouragement and sympathy and understanding.

JOHN D. ROCKEFELLER JR.

Love is not the saying of the words but the giving of the self.

ROBERT LANDER

........................................................................................................

........................................................................................................

........................................................................................................

........................................................................................................

# A Beautiful Life

Consider the lilies, how they grow: they neither toil nor spin;
and yet I say to you, even Solomon in all his glory
was not arrayed like one of these. If then God so clothes the grass,
which today is in the field and tomorrow is thrown
into the oven, how much more will He clothe you?

LUKE 12:27–28 NKJV


Something deep in all of us yearns for God's beauty,
and we can find it no matter where we are.

SUE MONK KIDD


Beauty puts a face on God. When we gaze at nature,
at a loved one, at a work of art, our soul immediately recognizes
and is drawn to the face of God.

MARGARET BROWNLEY


May God give you eyes to see beauty
only the heart can understand.

....................................................................................................

....................................................................................................

....................................................................................................

....................................................................................................

....................................................................................................

....................................................................................................

# My Provider

I must simply be thankful, and I am, for all
the Lord has provided for me, whether big or
small in the eyes of someone else.

MABEL P. ADAMSON

Those who know God as their Father know the whole secret.
They are His heirs, and may enter now into possession
of all that is necessary for their present needs.

HANNAH WHITALL SMITH

You care for the land and water it;
you enrich it abundantly.
The streams of God are filled with water
to provide the people with grain,
for so you have ordained it.

PSALM 65:9 NIV

You can trust God right now to supply all your needs for today.
And if your needs are more tomorrow,
His supply will be greater also.

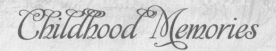

# Childhood Memories

Sooner or later we all discover that the important moments in life
are not the advertised ones, not the birthdays, the graduations,
the weddings, not the great goals achieved. The real milestones
are less prepossessing. They come to the door of memory.

SUSAN B. ANTHONY

How dear to the heart are the scenes of my childhood,
when fond recollection presents them to view.

SAMUEL WOODWORTH

I remember the days of long ago;
I meditate on all your works
and consider what your hands have done.

PSALM 143:5 NIV

Take the gift of this moment and make
something beautiful of it. Few worthwhile experiences
just happen, memories are made on purpose.

GLORIA GAITHER

...........................................................................................

...........................................................................................

...........................................................................................

...........................................................................................

...........................................................................................

# The Heart of Prayer

I said a prayer for you today
And I know God must have heard,
I felt the answer in my heart
Although He spoke no word.
I asked that He'd be near you
At the start of each new day,
To grant you health and blessings
And friends to share the way.
I asked for happiness for you
In all things great and small,
But it was His loving care
I prayed for most of all.

The God who made your children will hear your petitions.
He has promised to do so. After all, He loves them
more than you do.

JAMES DOBSON

As soon as I pray, you answer me;
you encourage me by giving me strength.

PSALM 138:3 NLT

..........................................................................................................

..........................................................................................................

..........................................................................................................

..........................................................................................................

# Be Encouraged

God, bless all young mothers at end of day.
Kneeling wearily with each small one to hear them pray.
Too tired to rise when done...and yet they do;
longing just to sleep one whole night through.
Too tired to sleep.... Too tired to pray....
God, bless all young mothers at close of day.

RUTH BELL GRAHAM

Being taken for granted can be a compliment.
It means that you've become a comfortable, trusted person
in another person's life.

JOYCE BROTHERS

Some days, it is enough encouragement just to watch the clouds
break up and disappear, leaving behind a blue patch of sky and
bright sunshine that is so warm upon my face.
It's a glimpse of divinity; a kiss from heaven.

The Scriptures give us hope and encouragement as we wait
patiently for God's promises to be fulfilled.

ROMANS 15:4 NLT

.....................................................................................................................

.....................................................................................................................

.....................................................................................................................

.....................................................................................................................

Ellie Claire™ Gift & Paper Corp.
Minneapolis, MN 55337
www.ellieclaire.com

*Words to Warm a Mother's Heart*
© 2012 by Ellie Claire™ Gift & Paper Corp.

ISBN 978-1-60936-638-4

Scripture references are from the following sources: The Holy Bible, New International Version®,
NIV®. Copyright © 1973, 1978, 1984, 2011 by Biblica, Inc.™ Used by permission of Zondervan.
All rights reserved worldwide. The Holy Bible, New King James Version (NKJV). Copyright © 1997, 1990,
1985, 1983 by Thomas Nelson, Inc. The New American Standard Bible® (NASB), copyright © 1960, 1962,
1963, 1968, 1971, 1972, 1973, 1975, 1977, 1995 by The Lockman Foundation. Used by permission.
The Holy Bible, New Living Translation (NLT), copyright 1996, 2004, 2007 by Tyndale House Foundation.
Used by permission of Tyndale House Publishers, Inc., Carol Stream, Illinois 60188. *The Message* (MSG).
Copyright © 1993, 1994, 1995, 1996, 2000, 2001, 2002 by Eugene Peterson. Used by permission of
NavPress, Colorado Springs, CO. The New Century Version® (NCV). Copyright © 1987, 1988, 1991,
2005 by Thomas Nelson, Inc. Used by permission. All rights reserved.

Excluding Scripture verses and deity pronouns, in some quotations references to men and masculine
pronouns have been replaced with gender-neutral or feminine references. Additionally, in some quotations
we have carefully updated verb forms and wording that may distract modern readers.

Stock or custom editions of Ellie Claire titles may be purchased in bulk for educational, business, ministry,
fundraising, or sales promotional use. For information, please e-mail specialmarkets@summersidepress.com.

Compiled by Barbara Farmer
Cover and interior design by Lisa and Jeff Franke

Printed in China

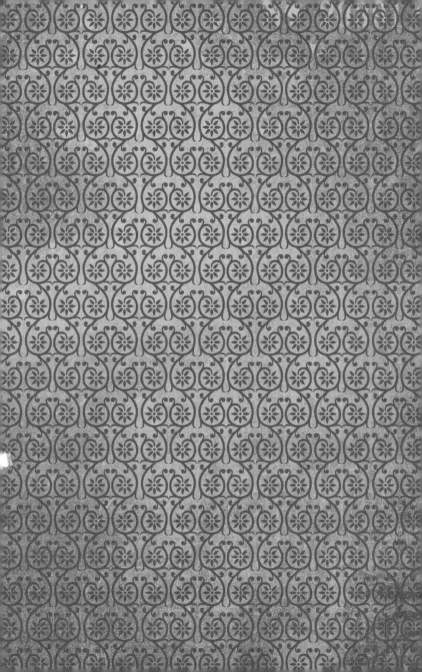